TV **COOKS**

Rick Stein

COOKS

Fish

Photographs by Philip Webb

BBC BOOKS

Published by BBC Books,
an imprint of BBC Worldwide Publishing.
BBC Worldwide Limited, Woodlands,
80 Wood Lane, London W12 0TT.

The majority of the recipes in this book
are adapted from recipes in:
Rick Stein's Taste of the Sea
© Richard Stein 1995

This edition first published 1997
Recipes © Rick Stein 1997
The moral right of the author has been asserted
Photographs by Philip Webb © BBC Consumer
Publishing 1997
Author photograph by Laurie Evans © BBC Consumer
Publishing 1997

ISBN 0 563 38344 5

Edited by Pam Mallender
Designed by DW Design
Stylist: Helen Payne
Home Economist: Fran Ward

Set in New Caledonia and Helvetica
Printed and bound in France by Imprimerie Pollina s.a.
Colour origination by Radstock Reproduction Ltd.
Midsomer Norton
Cover printed in France by Imprimerie Pollina·s.a.

Cover and frontispiece: Bouillabaisse

CONTENTS

RECIPE NOTES

Eggs are medium. If your kitchen is warm, keep the eggs in the fridge, but allow them to come to room temperature before using. While the proven risks of healthy people becoming ill from eating fresh raw eggs is minimal, pregnant women, the sick, the elderly and the very young should not do so just in case.

Wash all fresh produce before preparation and peel as necessary.

Spoon measurements are level. Always use proper measuring spoons:

1 teaspoon = 5ml and 1 tablespoon = 15ml.

Never mix metric and imperial measures in one recipe. Stick to one or the other.

HANDY CONVERSION TABLES

Weight		Volume		Linear	
15g	½oz	30ml	1fl oz	5mm	⅛in
25g	1oz	50ml	2fl oz	10mm/1cm	½in
40g	1½oz	100ml	3½fl oz	2cm	¾in
55g	2oz	125ml	4fl oz	2.5cm	1in
85g	3oz	150ml	5fl oz (¼ pint)	5cm	2in
115g	4oz	175ml	6fl oz	7.5cm	3in
140g	5oz	200ml	7fl oz (⅓ pint)	10cm	4in
175g	6oz	225ml	8fl oz	13cm	5in
200g	7oz	250ml	9fl oz	15cm	6in
225g	8oz	300ml	10fl oz (½ pint)	18cm	7in
250g	9oz	350ml	12fl oz	20cm	8in
280g	10oz	400ml	14fl oz	23cm	9in
350g	12oz	425ml	15fl oz (¾ pint)	25cm	10in
375g	13oz	450ml	16fl oz	28cm	11in
400g	14oz	500ml	18fl oz	30cm	12in
425g	15oz	600ml	20fl oz (1 pint)		
450g	1lb	700ml	1¼ pints		
550g	1¼lb	850ml	1½ pints		
750g	1lb 10oz	1 litre	1¾ pints		
900g	2lb	1.2 litres	2 pints		
1kg	2¼lb	1.3 litres	2¼ pints		
1.3kg	3lb	1.4 litres	2½ pints		
1.8kg	4lb	1.7 litres	3 pints		
2.25kg	5lb	2 litres	3½ pints		
		2.5 litres	4½ pints		

Oven temperatures

225F	110C	GAS ¼
250F	120C	GAS ½
275F	140C	GAS 1
300F	150C	GAS 2
325F	160C	GAS 3
350F	180C	GAS 4
375F	190C	GAS 5
400F	200C	GAS 6
425F	220C	GAS 7
450F	230C	GAS 8
475F	240C	GAS 9

(lf) **Low fat**

✳ **Suitable for freezing**

I'm really excited about this book for the simple reason that I didn't choose the recipes in it. All the recipes are mine, of course, and quite a few of them are new ones. The recipes were chosen by the BBC to give an objective view about what my cooking is all about. Suddenly, by reading it, I realised what my cooking is all about! Writing recipes is like any creative activity in that it is such a personal sort of thing that you sometimes think nobody else could possibly like that particular dish.

Reading through the book all the recipes seem simple and they all look fresh and inviting. As I read through the choice, I said to myself, Carpaccio of Monkfish with Lemon Olive Oil, that's a good one. Steamed Scallops with Ginger, Soya, Sesame and Spring Onions, such a great Chinese seafood dish. What about Mussel, Leek and Saffron Soup; that recipe was in my very first book *English Seafood Cookery*; it was great. We still serve it in the restaurant.

Some of the new recipes I've written are great classic dishes that I've never put in a book before like Seafood Gratin and Sole Normande. Perhaps the most exciting dish in the whole book for me is one that we're just putting on the menu in the restaurant because it's so simple and clean and good – Grilled Lemon Sole with Lemon Grass Butter.

I hope you like all the recipes. I think, above all, in a short inexpensive book with lots of pictures, you've got a really comprehensive coverage of everything that's bright, cheerful and exciting about modern fish cookery. You could almost call it The Bluffers Guide to Fish Cookery!

Rick Stein

INGREDIENTS

Butter Most of my cooking is done with unsalted butter these days. This is because salted butter tends to increase the amount of salt in a recipe and because I prefer the flavour. Nevertheless, sometimes it doesn't really matter which you use, in which case the recipe will just say butter. Salted butter is still significantly cheaper than unsalted because it keeps much better.

Chillies I've used Dutch chillies throughout this book because the heat factor is consistent. If you are not able to get hold of these, bite the very end off the tip of the chilli you use to taste the strength before using.

Flat fish We have in our waters the greatest range of flat fish anywhere in the world – from the regal turbot down to the humble dab.
Brill: as with all flat fish, if you're buying fillets, go for the larger fish. In the case of brill these should be about 1.3–3.5kg/3–8lb.
Plaice: of all sea fish, plaice has the closest flavour to freshwater fish. It is an attractive fish with almost fluorescent orange and red spots.

Fresh herbs *Dill:* these feathery leaves have a distinctive flavour with slight aniseed overtones.
Flatleaf parsley: this has a more pronounced flavour than the curly variety and is less bitter.
Thyme: full of an intensely aromatic essential oil, this is one of the most indispensable and popular herbs.

Olive oil In the recipes, I specify olive oil for general cooking when the flavour and expense of a fine olive oil would be wasted. I specify extra virgin olive oil when the aromatic flavours of a good oil are all-important. By olive oil I mean general purpose blended olive oil, by extra virgin I mean oil produced by the first cold pressing of the fruit. I tend to go for a good extra virgin Italian oil for using warm in my fish dishes and a French extra virgin for salad dressings. Italian tends to be stronger and more vigorous in flavour, the French softer and more subtle.

Shellfish *Langoustines:* these are also known as Dublin Bay prawns and are much more akin to lobsters than prawns. They look like lobsters and, like lobsters, their flesh deteriorates very quickly after death, becoming soft like cotton wool. To tell if they are really fresh, pull back their tails; if they have a good degree of spring the meat inside will be firm. If the tail stays spread out when you pull it, the meat will be soft. They should also smell sweet and appetising; avoid any with a suggestion of sourness or, worse still, ammonia.
Oysters: there are two types on sale in Britain, the Native and the Pacific, with the Native or European oyster usually costing about twice as much as the Pacific. The Native fetches a high price because it takes much longer to grow; the faster-growing Pacific is favoured by commercial growers. In a recent taste test I attended, the Natives won hands down. While the Pacifics were fresh and sweet, the Natives had a sort of slightly bitter, metallic finish to them which, in the end, proved subtle and exciting. Like a good wine, the complexities of the taste ended up being far more satisfying than the simple, straightforward flavours of the Pacific.
Winkles: I don't think I've ever seen winkles on sale in a fishmonger's shop in Britain. But they're very easy to pick on the sea shore. Turn over the seaweed on any rocky beach and you'll find winkles underneath. They come in various colours: yellow or a browny green but normally black or grey. They are all the same species and edible. Wash them in cold water, bring to the boil in well-salted water, then boil for 2 minutes. Drain and eat.

Thai fish sauce I use the South-east Asia anchovy essence called Thai fish sauce or *nam pla* in a large number of recipes. It has a clean salty taste and I like to use it in place of salt because it enhances flavours without actually being noticeable itself. I use a brand called Squid which we have found to have the cleanest taste. It also seems to be the type most easily found in Britain. Thai fish sauce has a much better flavour when it has been recently manufactured. You can tell how old it is simply by checking its colour. It is always dark brown but the fresher it is, the lighter the brown. If you can't get hold of fish sauce, use salt. Alternatively, you can use anchovy essence.

White peppercorns Peppercorns are the berries of a tropical vine. White peppercorns are fully-ripened berries which have had their red skin and outer flesh removed and are then dried. They are hot but less fragrant than black pepper.

EQUIPMENT

Cast-iron ribbed grill pan Essential for all char-grilled dishes.

Conical strainer I would earnestly suggest you buy a conical strainer and a ladle for passing soups and stock through, and a length of muslin through which you can pass sauces.

Deep-fat fryer Fish should be cooked between 180C/350F and 195C/380F. Deep-fat fryers are temperature-controlled, ensuring the oil is at the correct heat to successfully cook the fish.

Fish filleting knife Even if you buy all your fish filleted from the fishmonger there will still be occasions when you want to, say, remove some skin or slide a thin-bladed knife between the two shells of a scallop.

Fish kettle If you are serious about fish cookery this is a must. It also doubles as a steamer if you raise the perforated plate on stands such as two egg cups and bring a couple of inches of water in the bottom to the boil.

Fish scaler This is a wise investment if you are going to cook a lot of fish and it makes a messy job much easier.

Kitchen scissors Invaluable for trimming off sharp fins and tidying up tails.

Long-nosed pliers A small pair of these or tweezers for extracting bones from fillets of fish will make life infinitely easier.

Mandolin This is an unbelievably sharp vegetable slicer consisting of one or more metal blades fixed in a frame that can be supported in a tilted position. Not only can you slice potatoes wafer thin but it also makes the thinnest of julienne vegetables.

Mortar and pestle Perhaps the most valued piece of equipment I have in my kitchen at home. Ideal when you only want to grind or purée small quantities of fresh spices or crush a few peppercorns or garlic cloves. On these occasions a liquidiser or food processor is too big.

Salad spinner Ideal for washing and drying herbs as well as salads. Coriander and parsley both tend to be dusty and gritty and particularly benefit from being washed and dried.

1. Whole sea trout
2. Squid
3. Swordfish steaks
4. Whole herrings
5. Tuna fillet
6. Monkfish fillets
7. Fresh thyme
8. Fresh dill
9. Fresh flatleaf parsley
10. Fresh bay leaves
11. Thai fish sauce
12. Large cooked North Atlantic prawns
13. Fresh whelks
14. Fresh mussels
15. Fresh white crab meat
16. Fresh scallops
17. Langoustines
18. Fresh cockles
19. Fresh oysters
20. Cod fillets
21. Hake fillet
22. Canned butter beans
23. Dried butter beans
24. Fresh fennel bulb
25. White peppercorns
26. Saffron strands and powder
27. Fresh horseradish
28. Whole sea bass
29. Whole plaice
30. Brill fillets
31. Red mullet fillets
32. Fresh whole salmon cleaned and sliced in half for gravlax
33. Skate wing
34. Capers

1. Steamer
2. Expanding petal-shaped perforated steamer
3. Lobster picks
4. Salad spinner
5. Deep-fat fryer
6. Pepper grinders filled with white and black peppercorns
7. Pestle and mortar
8. Tweezers
9. Mandolin
10. Ladle
11. Fish scaler
12. Kitchen knife
13. Kitchen scissors
14. Oyster knife
15. Cast-iron ribbed grill pan
16. Muslin
17. Conical strainer
18. Fish kettle

Soups

MUSSEL, LEEK AND SAFFRON SOUP

This soup is quite special and is a classic dish. It comes from my first fish cookery book *English Seafood Cookery*, published by Penguin.

Serves 4

1.3kg/3lb or 1.7 litres/3 pints mussels

50ml/2fl oz white wine

85g/3oz unsalted butter

450g/1lb leeks, chopped, plus 5cm/2in piece of leek, cut into matchsticks, to serve

1 small onion, chopped

20g/¾oz plain flour

450ml/16fl oz Fish stock (page 62)

good pinch saffron

50ml/2fl oz double cream

Salt and freshly ground white pepper

1 Wash the mussels thoroughly, scraping off any barnacles, pulling out the beards and discarding any that are open and don't close when given a good tap. Place in a large pan and add a dash of the wine. Cover tightly and cook over a high heat for 3–4 minutes or until the mussels have opened, shaking the pan frequently.

2 Strain the cooking liquor and mussels through a colander into a bowl, shaking the colander well to drain off all the juices lodged in the shells. Reserve the liquor. Pull any remaining beards from the mussels and remove the meat from all but 12 of the shells.

3 Melt the butter in a pan and add the chopped leeks and onion. Cook over a low heat for 3 minutes. Stir in the flour until smooth. Gradually add the mussel liquor, remaining wine and fish stock to the pan, stirring until smooth. Bring to a simmer, then add a good pinch of saffron and cook for 25 minutes.

4 Meanwhile, blanch the leek matchsticks in a little salted water. Process the soup in a liquidiser or food processor, then strain through a sieve into a clean pan. Stir the cream into the soup and reheat. Just before serving add the mussel meats, the 12 mussels in their shells, the leek matchsticks and some seasoning and heat through gently.

Nutrition notes per serving: *345 calories, Protein 18g, Carbohydrate 9g, Fat 26g, Saturated fat 15g, Fibre 3g, Added sugar none, Salt 0.83g.*

TIP

There is no need to steep mussels in buckets of cold water with or without oatmeal. Not only is this totally ineffective but more likely to kill them than anything else. None of the water in the bucket will get inside the mussels, which will remain tightly closed. Mussels only open their shells when they sense that they're in well aerated water, sea water or brackish water.

BOUILLABAISSE

Fish stews, such as *bouillabaisse*, are wonderful for parties where everyone can sit around a large, deep tureen filled with all kinds of fish, adding lots of *rouille* to their bowls and mopping up the rich aromatic *bouillon* juices with crusty bread.

Serves 8–10

90ml/3fl oz olive oil, for frying

2 onions, roughly chopped

white of 2 large leeks, roughly chopped

4 celery sticks, thinly sliced

2 large fennel bulbs, thinly sliced

10 garlic cloves, chopped

2 x 5cm/2in pieces orange peel

900g/2lb tomatoes, skinned and chopped

½ red chilli, seeded and chopped

1 tsp saffron strands

2 fresh thyme sprigs

4 fresh bay leaves

3.5kg/7lb fish selection (See Tip)

675g/1½lb or 850ml/1½ pints mussels, washed and scraped clean

1 tsp roughly chopped fresh fennel herb (optional)

1 tsp chopped fresh oregano

1 tsp chopped fresh thyme

2 tbsp Pernod or Ricard

675g/1½lb shellfish, sliced

30ml/1fl oz extra virgin olive oil

cayenne pepper (optional)

salt and freshly ground black pepper

115g/4oz *Rouille* (See Tip), to serve

FOR THE CROUTONS

olive oil, for frying

12 thin slices French bread

2–3 garlic cloves

1 Make the *croûtons*: heat the oil in a frying pan and fry the bread slices on both sides until golden. Rub each slice with garlic, set aside and keep warm.

2 Make the *bouillabaisse*: heat the olive oil in a pan large enough to hold all the fish and 3.4 litres/6 pints of water. Add the onions, leeks, celery, fennel and garlic and cook until soft. Season with black pepper, then add the orange peel, tomatoes, chilli, saffron, thyme, bay leaves and 3.4 litres (6 pints) water and bring to the boil. Simmer for 10 minutes.

3 Add the fish, placing the firmer-fleshed fish such as conger eel, dogfish and skate in first. Add the softer fish 3 minutes later and the mussels 1 minute after that. While adding the fish, add the herbs and the Pernod. Continue to boil only until the fish is just cooked (about 8 minutes).

4 Add the shellfish and boil for 1 minute. Strain the soup through a colander and place all the fish, mussels, shellfish and vegetables in a large warm dish. Leave the mussels and shellfish in their shells. Set aside and keep warm.

5 Return the strained *bouillon* to the pan, add the oil and concentrate the flavour by rapid boiling. Check seasoning and add cayenne pepper if you like it (I do). Pour the *bouillon* over the fish and vegetables and scatter over the *croûtons*. You can separate the fish from the soup as they often do in France, if you prefer, but I like to eat them together served with a dollop of *rouille*.

Nutrition notes per serving: *954 calories, Protein 94g, Carbohydrate 30g, Fat 51g, Saturated fat 7g, Fibre 5g, Added sugar none, Salt 3.58g.*

TIP

You could use wrasse, dogfish, black bream, red bream, monkfish, cod, hake, weaver, trigger fish, gurnard, red mullet, bass, John Dory, bream, skate, congor eel, grey mullet. The more variety the better. For the shellfish choose between lobster, crayfish, langoustine or prawns in their shells. For the *rouille*: place 25g/1oz of dry bread soaked in fish stock, three garlic cloves, one egg yolk, two tablespoons harissa and a quarter teaspoon of salt in a food processor and blend. Gradually pour 225ml (8 fl oz) olive oil until it is incorporated with the egg yolk. For a quick *rouille* mix together mayonnaise, crushed garlic and seeded, chopped red chillies.

Starters

DEEP-FRIED GOUJONS OF LEMON SOLE WITH TARTARE SAUCE

Goujons are small pieces of skinned fish fillet, cut to about the size of a little finger, coated in breadcrumbs, then deep-fried. We use a Japanese breadcrumb called *panko*, which fries much crisper than any other coating. However, you can still get perfectly acceptable results making these with ordinary fresh breadcrumbs; they make a perfect first course and are universally popular.

Serves 4

350g/12oz skinless lemon sole fillet

25g/1oz seasoned flour

2 eggs, beaten

55g/2oz *panko* or fresh breadcrumbs

1 lemon, cut into wedges, to serve

FOR THE TARTARE SAUCE

1 quantity Mustard mayonnaise (See Tip)

1 tsp green olives, finely chopped

1 tsp gherkins, finely chopped

1 tsp capers, finely chopped

1 tsp snipped fresh chives

1 tsp chopped fresh parsley

1 Make the tartare sauce: mix all the ingredients together. Cut the lemon sole into *goujons*: slice the fillet diagonally to make long pieces about the size of your little finger.

2 Place the flour in a small shallow dish or tray. Place the eggs in a second dish or tray and place the breadcrumbs in a third.

3 Set the deep-fat fryer to 190C/375F, or heat some oil in a large pan to the same temperature or until a cube of bread browns in about 30 seconds. If it blackens in the same time it is too hot.

4 Dip the *goujons* first in the seasoned flour, then the egg and finally the breadcrumbs, then deep-fry until golden. Drain on kitchen paper. Serve with the lemon wedges and Tartare sauce.

Nutrition notes per serving: *821 calories, Protein 23g, Carbohydrate 13g, Fat 76g, Saturated fat 14g, Fibre 1g, Added sugar 0.01g, Salt 2g.*

TIP

To make Mustard mayonnaise, ensure all the ingredients are at room temperature before starting. You will need: one tablespoon English mustard; two egg yolks; one tablespoon white wine vinegar; three-quarters teaspoon salt; few turns of white pepper; and 300ml/½ pint groundnut or sunflower oil. Place the mustard, egg yolks, vinegar, salt and pepper in a mixing bowl, then place the bowl on a tea towel to stop it slipping. Using a wire whisk, beat the oil into the egg mixture a little at a time until it is all incorporated. Once you have carefully added about the same volume of oil as the original mixture of egg yolks and vinegar, you can add the oil more quickly.

CAUTION! The sauce in this recipe contains raw eggs.

MOULES À LA CRÈME

This is just *Moules Marinières* with cream in it, but it adds a little bit of extra sparkle that's sometimes just what's needed. Delicious served with plenty of crusty French bread.

Serves 4

1.8kg/4lb fresh mussels

225ml/8fl oz dry cider, Normandy if possible

3 shallots or 1 small onion, very finely chopped

1 bouquet garni (bay leaf, parsley stalks, thyme sprigs)

25g/1oz butter, softened

15g/½oz plain flour

150ml/¼ pint crème fraîche

2 tbsp chopped fresh parsley

salt and freshly ground black pepper

1 Scrub the mussels and pull out the beards protruding from between the closed shells. Discard any mussels that won't stay closed.

2 Place the cider, shallots, bouquet garni and plenty of freshly ground black pepper in a large pan, bring to the boil, then simmer for 2 minutes.

3 Add the mussels, cover the pan and cook over a high heat for 3–4 minutes until the mussels have opened. Discard any that remain closed. Using a slotted spoon, transfer the mussels into a large, deep serving dish, discarding the bouquet garni, cover and keep hot. Reserve the cooking juices.

4 Mix the butter with the flour to make a smooth paste. Bring the reserved cooking juices to the boil, add the crème fraîche, then whisk in the butter paste a little piece at a time. Simmer the sauce very gently for 5 minutes to cook out the flour. Taste the sauce for seasoning, stir in the chopped parsley and then pour it all over the mussels

Nutrition notes per serving: *312 calories, Protein 18g, Carbohydrate 6g, Fat 23g, Saturated fat 13g, Fibre 1g, Added sugar none, Salt 1.39g.*

A SALAD OF PLAICE WITH GINGER, LIME AND CHILLI

This ceviche of plaice is perfectly off-set, I think, by a line of wafer-thin slices of beef tomatoes dressed with a little extra virgin olive oil and salt.

Serves 4

350g/12oz skinless plaice fillets

2 limes

1cm/½in piece fresh root ginger, peeled and very finely chopped

2 red bird's eye chillies, seeded and very finely chopped (See Tip)

1 tbsp chopped fresh coriander

2 small beefsteak tomatoes, very thinly sliced

extra virgin olive oil

1 tsp salt

1 Cut the plaice fillets into long thin strips about the thickness of your little finger, then place in a shallow non-metallic dish.

2 Coarsely grate the rind from half of one lime, then squeeze the juices from both. Pour over the fish and add the ginger, chillies, chopped coriander and salt. Mix well, cover and chill for 3 hours.

3 Spoon the plaice on to one side of each plate. Arrange a line of overlapping tomato slices on the other side, then sprinkle them with a little olive oil and salt and garnish with the coriander sprigs.

Nutrition notes per serving: *118 calories, Protein 16g, Carbohydrate 2g, Fat 5g, Saturated fat 1g, Fibre 1g, Added sugar none, Salt 0.53g.*

TIP

Take care when preparing chillies. Wash your hands, knife and chopping board thoroughly afterwards and do not touch your eyes for a while.

PRAWN COCKTAIL WITH MALT WHISKY

There is no substitute for tomato ketchup in the sauce, and the yogurt adds a subtle tartness.

TV Cooks RICK STEIN COOKS FISH

Serves 4

225g/8oz cooked large peeled frozen North Atlantic prawns, thawed if frozen

FOR THE MARIE ROSE SAUCE

2 egg yolks

2 tsp white wine vinegar

pinch ground white pepper

¼ tsp salt

225ml/8fl oz vegetable oil

5 tbsp tomato ketchup

2 tbsp single malt whisky

4 tbsp natural unsweetened yogurt

FOR THE SALAD

100g/3½oz mixed salad leaves, including radicchio, if possible

4 fresh basil leaves, thinly sliced

1 Chill four large glasses. Make the sauce: whisk together the egg yolks, vinegar, pepper and salt. Continue whisking and gradually drizzle in the oil to make a mayonnaise. Stir in the tomato ketchup, whisky and yogurt.

2 Tear the salad leaves into pieces not more than 5cm/2in across and divide between glasses, then top with the prawns, leaving a gap around the circumference of the glass.

3 Spoon over the sauce without totally covering the prawns and leaves. Place a little pile of sliced basil leaves in the centre of each glass.

Nutrition notes per serving: *549 calories, Protein 16g, Carbohydrate 6g, Fat 50g, Saturated fat 6g, Fibre 1g, Added sugar 3g, Salt 3.11g.*

CAUTION! This recipe contains raw eggs.

CARPACCIO OF MONKFISH WITH LEMON OLIVE OIL

This recipe was given to me by head chef, Paul Ripley.

Serves 4

225g/8oz monkfish fillet

50ml/2fl oz Lemon olive oil (See Tip)

salt and freshly ground white pepper

55g/2oz rocket leaves

15g/½oz Parmesan

1 To thinly slice the monkfish fillet, you will need to partly freeze it. Freeze for about 1 hour, then using your sharpest, thinnest knife, thinly slice.

2 Lay the slices on four cold plates, pour over the lemon olive oil and dust lightly with salt and pepper.

3 Top with the rocket leaves and, using a potato peeler, make shavings from the Parmesan. Lay six to eight shavings over the rocket leaves, then serve.

Nutrition notes per serving: *141 calories, Protein 10g, Carbohydrate 0.06g, Fat 11g, Saturated fat 2g, Fibre trace, Added sugar none, Salt 0.39g.*

TIP

For Lemon olive oil: carefully pare the rind from one lemon with a potato peeler. Slice the rind into thin strips, then add to 600ml/1 pint of extra virgin olive oil. Leave to infuse for 12 hours. You can also buy a brand of extra virgin olive oil with natural essence of lemons which is superb for salads.

Main Courses

POACHED SALMON WITH MAYONNAISE, NEW POTATOES AND CUCUMBER SALAD

Well-produced farmed salmon is perfectly acceptable for this dish but even more delightful is wild salmon. I'd far sooner you cooked with farmed fish, than not at all. If you prefer, you can use sea trout, a brown trout which has exchanged its habitat of rivers for the open sea. Its flesh develops a pink colour from a diet of crustaceans but is slightly less pronounced than salmon. Salmon and sea trout taste far better if eaten slightly underdone than overcooked, and if using in this recipe should be served warm not hot.

Serves 4

1 x 1.3–1.6kg/3–3½lb salmon or sea trout

675g/1½lb new potatoes

3 fresh mint sprigs

1 cucumber

1 tbsp white wine vinegar

1 quantity Olive oil mayonnaise (page 62)

FOR THE COURT-BOUILLON

½ lemon, thinly sliced

2 bay leaves

150ml/¼ pint white wine vinegar

1 carrot, thinly sliced

1 onion, thinly sliced

12 black peppercorns

5 tbsp salt

1 Place all the court-bouillon ingredients and 3.4 litres/6 pints in a fish kettle and bring to the boil, then simmer for 10 minutes. (See Tip for an alternative way of cooking if you do not have a fish kettle.)

2 Add the salmon, bring back to the boil and simmer very gently for 5 minutes. Remove the fish kettle from the heat and set aside to cool for about 20 minutes.

3 Boil the new potatoes in salted water with one sprig of mint until soft, then drain and keep warm. Peel the cucumber and slice as thinly as possible, preferably using a mandolin (see page 7).

4 Chop the leaves of the remaining mint sprigs and mix with the cucumber slices and wine vinegar. Remove the salmon from the fish kettle and serve with the new potatoes, cucumber salad and mayonnaise.

Nutrition notes per serving: *1013 calories, Protein 42g, Carbohydrate 29g, Fat 82g, Saturated fat 15g, Fibre 2g, Added sugar 0.01g, Salt 1.28g.*

TIP

A fish up to 1.6kg/3½lb will normally fit into a large oval casserole dish if you bend it. Or, you could remove the head and tail and fit it into your largest pan.

FISH CAKES ✳

I have included anchovy essence in this recipe because it improves the flavour dramatically. You can also use Thai fish sauce (*nam pla*) if you prefer, or just add more salt.

Serves 4

450g/1lb mashed potatoes, cooled

2 eggs

25g/1oz melted butter

2 tsp anchovy essence or Thai fish sauce (*nam pla*)

2 tbsp chopped fresh parsley

1 tsp salt

10 turns black pepper mill

450g/1lb cooked white fish (See Tip), broken into small pieces with skin and bones removed

55g/2oz seasoned flour

2 eggs, beaten

150g/5½oz fresh white breadcrumbs

oil, for frying

1 Mix the potatoes with the eggs and melted butter, then fold in the anchovy essence, parsley, salt and pepper and fish pieces.

2 Shape the mixture into fish cakes, using your hands and a palette knife. Coat each cake in flour, then beaten egg, then breadcrumbs. Shallow or deep fry, as you prefer until crisp and golden and heated right through.

Nutrition notes per serving: *652 calories, Protein 37g, Carbohydrate 48g, Fat 36g, Saturated fat 8g, Fibre 3g, Added sugar none, Salt 3.02g.*

✳ *These can be frozen, cooked or uncooked, for up to 1 month. Defrost thoroughly before cooking or reheating, covered, until piping hot.*

TIP

You can use any white fish or, indeed, any oily fish to make these fish cakes but cheaper white fish such as ling, coley, pollack, whiting and pouting (also known as pout or bib) are ideal.

HAKE AND POTATO PIE WITH A GARLIC, PARSLEY AND BREADCRUMB CRUST ✳

I'm very fond of this simple French fish pie. Hake has a fine flavour and a soft, milky texture.

Serves 4

450g/1lb potatoes, cut into 5mm/¼in slices

115g/4oz butter

450g/1lb skinless hake fillet, cut into 2.5cm/1in thick slices

2 slices white bread

2 garlic cloves

15g/½oz fresh parsley

salt and freshly ground black pepper

1 Preheat the oven to 200C/400F/Gas 6. Parboil the potatoes for 2 minutes, then drain. Grease an ovenproof dish with half the butter.

2 Layer the hake and potato slices in the dish finishing with a layer of potatoes. Season and dot with remaining butter. Cover and bake for 15 minutes, basting with the butter twice.

3 Place the bread, garlic and parsley in a food processor or liquidiser and process to crumbs. Season, then sprinkle over the pie and bake, uncovered, for 15 minutes or until crisp.

Nutrition notes per serving: *421 calories, Protein 24g, Carbohydrate 27g, Fat 25g, Saturated fat 15g, Fibre 2g, Added sugar none, Salt 1.24g.*

✳ *Freeze the pie in its dish for up to 1 month. Defrost thoroughly, then reheat, covered, until piping hot.*

ROAST SEA BASS WITH BRAISED RED CABBAGE AND RÖSTI POTATOES

An ideal dish for the cooler months. Sea bass easily justifies its high price. Soft in texture with a sweet delicate flavour, it never fails to delight, particularly when it is cooked in a way that crisps up the skin.

Serves 4

1 x 1.6kg/3½lb sea bass

melted butter, for brushing

½ tsp salt

freshly ground black pepper

FOR THE RED CABBAGE

280g/10oz red cabbage

175g/6oz unsalted butter

150ml/¼ pint Fish stock (page 62) or chicken stock

115g/4oz onion, diced

150ml/¼ pint red wine

30ml/1fl oz wine vinegar

1 tsp salt

1 tbsp sugar

FOR THE RÖSTI POTATOES

400g/14oz potatoes

25g/1oz smoked bacon or pancetta, cut into thin strips

50ml/2fl oz clarified butter, for frying

1 Preheat the oven to 200C/400F/Gas 6. Make the braised cabbage: remove the outer leaves and cut out the thick white core. Slice as thinly as possible, then cut the slices into the smallest possible pieces. Place the cabbage in an ovenproof dish with 55g/2oz of butter, half the stock and remaining cabbage ingredients. Cover and cook for 1¼ hours, stirring occasionally. Remove from the oven, add the remaining stock, bring to the boil and stir in the remaining butter. Keep warm. Turn the oven to its highest setting.

2 Make the rösti: peel the potatoes and shred on the largest grid of a grater on to a clean tea towel. Gather the edges of the tea towel and squeeze as much moisture out of the potatoes as you can. (Don't rinse the potatoes or you will remove the starch that binds them into a pancake.) Season the potatoes and add the bacon. Divide into four and shape into balls using your hands.

3 Pour the clarified butter into a small non-stick or well-tempered frying pan and add one potato ball. Flatten it to about 10cm/4in in diameter using a fish slice. Fry over a gentle heat for 5 minutes. Turn over and cook for 5 minutes on the other side. Towards the end of cooking time, press out, then pour off excess butter. Drain on kitchen paper and keep warm. Repeat for the other rösti.

4 Brush the bass inside and out with the melted butter, then season inside and out. Place in a roasting tin and roast for 25 minutes basting a couple of times with the juices from the tray. Place the fish on an oval platter and pour over the pan juices. Serve with the cabbage and rösti potatoes.

Nutrition notes per serving: *883 calories, Protein 61g, Carbohydrate 26g, Fat 57g, Saturated fat 32g, Fibre 3g, Added sugar 4g, Salt 2.84g.*

TIP

The object of subjecting the bass to such a fierce heat is to crisp the skin on the outside while cooking the inside as quickly as possible. This method of cooking is also successful for thick fillets of fish, thick *tronçons* (slices of flat fish cut on the bone such as turbot or brill) and other whole fish.

CLASSIC SOLE NORMANDE

There are hundreds of recipes for whole Dover sole or lemon sole poached with a little cider, fish stock and flavouring ingredients but this, in my opinion, is the best. One of the real problems of eating whole flat fish are all those tiny little bones that run along the sides of them. In this recipe, all those bones are simply removed after cooking so that all you are left with is four fillets and the backbone, making it easy to eat. Serve with boiled new potatoes.

Serves 4

4 x 300–350g/10–12oz Dover or lemon sole (See Tip)

24 shell-on North Atlantic prawns

450ml/¾ pint Fish stock (page 62)

350g/12oz fresh mussels, cleaned

2 shallots, very thinly sliced

175g/6oz button mushrooms, wiped and thinly sliced

90ml/3fl oz dry cider (Normandy if possible)

25g/1oz butter, softened

20g/¾oz plain flour

2 egg yolks

150ml/¼ pint double cream

1 tbsp chopped fresh parsley

salt and freshly ground black pepper

1 Preheat the oven to 190C/375F/Gas 5. Skin the darker side and scale the lighter side of the Dover sole, if using, and trim off the fins from either fish. Peel all but eight of the prawns.

2 Place the fish stock in a pan and bring to the boil. Add the mussels, cover and cook over a high heat for 3–4 minutes, until the mussels have opened. Discard any that remain closed. Tip them into a sieve set over a bowl. Reserve the stock. Remove the meats from all but eight of the mussel shells.

3 Sprinkle the shallots and mushrooms over the base of a shallow ovenproof dish or roasting tin, large enough to take the fish side by side in one layer (they can overlap very slightly if need be). Place the fish on top and season. Pour over all but the last tablespoon of stock (this might contain a little sand from the mussels) and the cider. Cover with foil and bake for 15 minutes.

4 Lift the fish on to a board. Remove the side bones by dragging them out with the blade of a sharp knife – they will pull out quite easily. Transfer the fish to four warmed plates, garnish with the mussels in their shells and the unpeeled prawns and set aside. Preheat the grill to its highest setting.

5 Melt the butter in a pan. Stir in the flour and cook for 30 seconds. Take the pan off the heat and gradually stir in the cooking juices and vegetables from the baking dish. Bring to the boil, stirring, and simmer for 10–15 minutes.

6 Mix the egg yolks with the cream, stir into the sauce and simmer for 1–2 minutes until it coats the back of a spoon. Stir in the shelled prawns, mussels and parsley and season. Spoon sauce over each fish and slide each one under the grill for 1–2 minutes until sauce is lightly flecked with brown.

Nutrition notes per serving: 490 calories, Protein 48g, Carbohydrate 6g, Fat 30g, Saturated fat 17g, Fibre trace, Added sugar none, Salt 2.26g.

TIP

Lemon sole is well-suited to serving with sauces. It seems to have a particularly sweet affinity with cream, fish stock and white wine.

SALMON MARINATED IN DILL

The best cut of salmon for this dish, known in Scandinavia as gravlax, is the middle of the fish. Ask your fishmonger to cut the salmon in half lengthways and remove the bones. Wash and scale it before beginning the marinating (See Tip).

Serves 6

1.25kg/2¾lb fresh salmon

1 large bunch fresh dill

115g/4oz salt, preferably sea salt

85g/3oz sugar

2 tbsp white peppercorns, crushed

1 Place half the fish, skin side down, in a shallow dish. Roughly chop the dill and mix it with the salt, sugar and white pepper. Cover the salmon with this dry cure and place the other piece of salmon on top, skin side up.

2 Cover with foil or plastic film and place a plate, slightly bigger than the salmon, on top. Place a weight on top of the plate to press the fish down. Keep in the fridge for two days, turning the fish about every 12 hours and spooning over juices. Replace the weight each time.

3 Remove the salmon from the brine and slice thinly. You can scrape off the dill coating if you like but I think it looks rather nice. Serve with the Horseradish and mustard sauce.

Nutrition notes per serving: *316 calories, Protein 31g, Carbohydrate 4g, Fat 20g, Saturated fat 5g, Fibre none, Added sugar 4g, Salt 3.38g.*

TIP

Scales are easier to remove while the fish is moist. If you let the skin dry at all, the scales are very hard to get off. Scaling is best done on several sheets of newspaper as scales tend to fly everywhere. Remove them by scraping the fish from tail to head using a blunt, thick-bladed knife, a special descaler or even a scallop shell. A descaler does the best job.

HORSERADISH AND MUSTARD SAUCE

This is the perfect accompaniment to the Salmon marinated in dill. It also goes well with smoked salmon.

Serves 6

2 tsp grated fresh horseradish

2 tsp grated onion, grated on a cheese grater

1 tsp Dijon mustard

1 tsp sugar

30ml/1fl oz white wine vinegar

good pinch salt

225ml/8fl oz double cream

1 Mix together all the ingredients except the cream. Whip the cream to stiff peaks, then fold in the remaining ingredients, cover and chill until needed.

Nutrition notes per serving: *193 calories, Protein 1g, Carbohydrate 2g, Fat 20g, Saturated fat 13g, Fibre trace, Added sugar 1g, Salt 0.52g.*

A CASSEROLE OF BRILL WITH SHALLOTS AND WILD MUSHROOMS

You can use either brill, turbot or large plaice for this dish. This recipe is definitely only for large fish as you need a good thick fillet for success.

15g/½oz dried ceps

100g/3½oz unsalted butter

½ tsp sugar

12 small shallots

8 garlic cloves

850ml/1½ pints chicken stock

¼ tsp salt

freshly ground black pepper

1 slice cooked ham, cut into fine dice

1 carrot, chopped

1 celery stick, chopped

1 leek, chopped

½ medium onion, chopped

2 tsp balsamic vinegar

2 fresh thyme sprigs

50ml/2fl oz red wine

675g/1½lb brill fillets, divided into 4 portions

100g/3½oz wild mushrooms, sliced (See Tip)

1 Soak the ceps for 30 minutes in 150ml/¼ pint warm water.

2 Use a shallow pan large enough to take the brill fillets in one layer. Melt 25g/1oz butter with the sugar, then add the shallots and garlic and cook until lightly browned. Barely cover with some of the chicken stock and add the salt and black pepper. Add the ham and simmer until the shallots and garlic are tender. Turn up the heat and reduce the stock to a thick syrupy glaze so that both the shallots and garlic are coated and become dark. Remove from the pan and keep warm. (Use the same pan, unwashed, to finish the dish so the syrupy juices combine with the rest of the sauce.)

3 Make a stock: fry the carrot, celery, leek and onion in 25g/1oz butter. Allow the vegetables to catch a little to create a rich brown finish to the sauce. Strain the soaking liquid from the ceps and add to the remaining chicken stock, the balsamic vinegar, a thyme sprig and the red wine and pour over the vegetables. Simmer for 20–30 minutes, then pass through a conical strainer into another pan.

4 Heat a frying pan and melt a little butter. Quickly brown the skin side of the brill, season and remove. Reserve the pan. Place the fillets in one layer in the pan used to cook the shallots and garlic and pour over the stock. Add remaining thyme, cover, and braise until the brill is just cooked.

5 Meanwhile, take the frying pan in which you first browned the brill, add 15g/½oz butter and fry all the mushrooms, then season.

6 Remove the brill from the pan and keep warm. Reduce the cooking liquid a little, then add the remaining butter and the mushrooms. Place the brill on to four plates with the glazed shallots and garlic and spoon over the sauce.

Nutrition notes per serving: *404 calories, Protein 36g, Carbohydrate 11g, Fat 24g, Saturated fat 12g, Fibre 3g, Added sugar 1g, Salt 1.60g.*

TIP

If you can't get wild mushrooms go for ordinary field mushrooms and maybe some shiitake and oyster mushrooms to provide variety.

SMOKED HADDOCK PASTIES WITH CLOTTED CREAM ✲

We sell these pasties in our delicatessen in Padstow. We sell out every day and they are, in my opinion, the ultimate fish pasty. Serve hot or cold.

Makes 6 pasties

900g/2lb chilled fresh puff pastry

350g/12oz skinless undyed smoked haddock, cut into 2.5cm/1in pieces

175g/6oz leeks, sliced

280g/10oz potatoes, cut into 1cm/½in cubes

4 tablespoons clotted cream

1 teaspoon salt

freshly ground black pepper

1 egg, beaten

1 Preheat the oven to 200C/400F/Gas 6. Roll out the pastry on a lightly floured surface and cut out six 19cm/7½in discs.

2 Make the filling: mix together the smoked haddock, leeks, potatoes, clotted cream, salt and pepper.

3 Divide the filling mixture between the circles of pastry. Moisten one half of the pastry edge with a little beaten egg, bring the sides together over the top of the filling and pinch together well to seal. Crimp the edge of each one decoratively between the fingers, lift on to a lightly greased baking sheet and brush all over with beaten egg. Bake for 35 minutes until crisp and golden.

Nutrition notes per serving: *737 calories, Protein 22g, Carbohydrate 65g, Fat 45g, Saturated fat 6g, Fibre 1g, Added sugar none, Salt 3.78g.*

✲ *These pasties can be frozen cooked or uncooked for up to 1 month. Defrost thoroughly before cooking or reheating covered, until piping hot.*

GRILLED LEMON SOLE WITH LEMON GRASS BUTTER

I can think of no better way of cooking lemon sole than to simply grill it.

Serves 4

1 lemon grass stalk, outside leaves removed and core very finely chopped

finely grated rind of ½ lime, plus 2 tsp juice

1cm/½in piece fresh root ginger, peeled and very finely chopped

2 tbsp chopped fresh parsley

125g/4½oz butter

1 tbsp Thai fish sauce

20 turns black pepper mill

4 x 350–450g/12 oz–1lb lemon sole

salt and freshly ground black pepper

1 Place the lemon grass, lime rind and juice, ginger, parsley, 115g/4oz butter, fish sauce and pepper in a food processor and blend until smooth. Spoon into a piece of plastic film, shape into a 4cm/1½in wide roll and chill until firm.

2 Preheat the grill to high. Melt remaining butter and brush the fish on both sides, then season. Grilll one or two at a time on a buttered baking tray or grill rack for 4½–5 minutes. Lift onto warmed serving plates and keep warm.

3 Cut off 16 thin slices of butter and lay four slices down the centre of each fish. Slide each plate briefly back under the grill until the butter just begins to melt.

Nutrition notes per serving: *419 calories, Protein 43g, Carbohydrate 1g, Fat 27g, Saturated fat 16g, Fibre trace, Added sugar none, Salt 1.80g.*

TIP

There will be a little more butter than you need for this dish but it will keep in the freezer for up to 2 months.

ROAST COD WITH AÏOLI AND BUTTER BEANS

This is the hot version of the classic Provençal dish *Aïoli Garni*. Cod doesn't have such a good flavour as other more expensive fish but there are some serious compensations to this. It has a satisfying chewy texture, enormous milky flakes and, with large cod, bones are not a problem because they are too obvious to be eaten accidentally.

Serves 4

55g/2oz dried butter beans (soaked overnight)

2 eggs

1 Florence fennel bulb

4 x 175–200g/6–7oz cod fillets with skin

melted butter, for brushing

6 fresh basil leaves, thinly sliced

1 tsp sea salt

freshly ground black pepper

1 quantity *Aïoli* (See Tip)

FOR THE SAUCE

225g/8oz chopped mixed carrot, leek, celery and onion

55g/2oz unsalted butter

1 tbsp cognac

10g/¼oz dried mushrooms

1 tbsp balsamic vinegar

¼ red chilli

2 tbsp olive oil

1 tsp Thai fish sauce (*nam pla*)

600ml/1 pint Fish stock (page 62)

½ tsp salt

4 fresh basil leaves, finely sliced

1 Make the sauce: sweat the chopped mixed vegetables in a large pan with half the butter until soft. Add the cognac and let it boil, then add all the remaining sauce ingredients, except the remaining butter and basil leaves. Simmer for 30 minutes, then pass through a fine sieve. Bring the sauce back to the boil and simmer until it has reduced to about 150ml/¼ pint.

2 Bring the butter beans to the boil in a large pan of salted water. Simmer gently until very soft. Remove from the heat and keep warm in the cooking liquid.

3 Preheat the oven to 230C/450F/Gas 8. Place the eggs in boiling water and boil for 8 minutes, drain, remove the shells and keep warm.

4 Remove the outer leaves of the fennel but don't cut off the tops. Slice into thin sections, then cook in salted water until just tender. Drain and keep warm.

5 Roast the cod until just cooked through. (This will take 10–15 minutes depending on the thickness of the fillet.) Transfer to four plates. Drain the butter beans and divide between the plates. Add the fennel, cut the eggs in half and place one half on each plate, then add a spoonful of *aïoli*.

6 Bring the sauce to a boil and whisk in the remaining butter, then add the basil leaves. Pour the sauce over the butter beans, egg and fennel and serve.

Nutrition notes per serving: *965 calories, Protein 42g, Carbohydrate 16g, Fat 81g, Saturated fat 19g, Fibre 4g, Added sugar 0.01g, Salt 3.75g.*

TIP

For *Aïoli* you will need eight peeled and crushed garlic cloves and one quantity of Olive oil mayonnaise (page 62) mixed together. If you don't have a garlic crusher, mash a peeled clove with the large flat blade of a knife. Place the garlic on a firm, non-slip surface (a wooden chopping board is best), position the widest part of the knife on the garlic, then hit it with the palm of your hand. Chop, then sprinkle with salt and mash with the knife to a purée.

CAUTION! The aïoli contains raw eggs.

Crustaceans & Shellfish

CRAB AND BASIL TIMBALES WITH A SWEET AND SHARP TOMATO DRESSING

The crab is served at room temperature with a rich tomato sauce which is cooked until thick with some garlic and fresh basil.

Serves 4

350g/12oz white crab meat, preferably fresh

10 fresh basil leaves, very finely shredded

2 tbsp extra virgin olive oil

1 tbsp fresh lemon juice

salt and freshly ground black pepper

basil sprigs, to garnish

baby salad leaves, to serve

FOR THE TOMATO DRESSING

1 small onion, chopped

1 small garlic clove, chopped

6 tbsp olive oil

200g/7oz can chopped tomatoes

50ml/2fl oz red wine vinegar

2 tsp sugar

1 tbsp sherry vinegar

salt and freshly ground black pepper

1 Make the dressing: fry the onion and the garlic in one tablespoon of olive oil until soft. Add the chopped tomatoes and simmer for 30 minutes until very thick – you should be able to drag a spoon across the bottom of the pan and it should not run back, a bit like the parting of the Red Sea. Place the vinegar and sugar in a small pan and boil down to about one teaspoon. Add to the tomato sauce and leave to go cold. Season with salt and about 10 turns of black pepper.

2 Mix the crab meat, basil, olive oil and lemon juice together in a bowl. Season with salt and pepper. Line four lightly oiled 9cm (3½in) ramekins with a sheet of plastic film and spoon the crab mixture equally into each one and lightly press down.

3 Place the remaining oil for the dressing in a bowl with the sherry vinegar and whisk together. Stir in the tomato sauce and adjust the seasoning if necessary. Invert the timbales slightly off centre on to four plates and, using a teaspoon, spoon a little of the dressing around one side of each one. Place a pile of baby salad leaves alongside and serve garnished with the basil leaves.

Nutrition notes per serving: *336 calories, Protein 18g, Carbohydrate 6g, Fat 27g, Saturated fat 4g, Fibre 1g, Added sugar 3g, Salt 1.13g.*

TIP

A timbale is simply a particular type of round dish that we use at the restaurant in which to mould the crab and then turn it out into a pleasing shape on the plate, but a ramekin will do just as well.

HOT SHELLFISH WITH GARLIC AND LEMON JUICE

This Italian dish is a sort of hot *fruits de mer*. The quantities of shellfish are merely a suggestion. You may like to make this out of fewer or more varieties, or include crab or lobster as well to make it more substantial. I have given cooking methods for all the shellfish but you may find that you can more easily buy it ready cooked, in which case you will only need to warm it through.

Serves 4

4 whelks

32 winkles

8 cooked langoustine or 8 cooked Mediterranean prawns

24 mussels

dry white wine

20 cockles

4 large clams

16 small clams

8 oysters

90ml/3fl oz extra virgin olive oil

2 garlic cloves, finely chopped

small bunch fresh parsley, preferably flatleaf, roughly chopped

1 red chilli, seeded and finely chopped

juice of ½ lemon

1 Add the whelks to a pan of well-salted, boiling water, allow the water to return to the boil, then simmer for 4 minutes. Add the winkles to boiling, salted water, return to the boil, then drain at once. Keep both warm.

2 If you are using cooked winkles and whelks, place them in a pan, of well-salted, boiling water together with the cooked langoustine or prawns and warm them through.

3 Place the mussels in a large pan with a lid, and splash in some white wine. Place the pan over a fierce heat, cover and leave until they have opened. Remove with a slotted spoon and keep warm. Do the same with the cockles, the clams and the oysters, cooking them in the same pan, one after the other. The oysters will take longest and will not fully open; you will need to lever them open with a short, thick-bladed knife or oyster knife.

4 Strain the cooking liquor and the liquor from the oysters into a small pan through a fine sieve or muslin to remove any grit. Add the olive oil, garlic, parsley, chilli and lemon juice and bring to the boil. Arrange the shellfish on four large warmed plates or one very large serving dish and pour over the liquor. Serve with plenty of French bread or ciabatta.

Nutrition notes per serving: *277 calories, Protein 22g, Carbohydrate 2g, Fat 18g, Saturated fat 3g, Fibre 1g, Added sugar none, Salt 4.20g.*

STEAMED SCALLOPS WITH GINGER, SOY, SESAME AND SPRING ONIONS

This recipe came to me as a result of a visit to a Chinese restaurant in Gerrard Street, Soho.

Serves 4

16 scallops opened, cleaned and left in their bottom shells

1 tsp finely chopped fresh root ginger

125ml/4fl oz sesame oil

2 tbsp dark soy sauce

1 tbsp chopped fresh coriander

3 spring onions, finely sliced

1 Sprinkle the scallops with ginger. Place in a simple petal-shaped perforated steamer and steam for about 4 minutes until only just set. If you don't have a steamer, pour a couple of inches of boiling water into a large pan and place some sort of trivet in the bottom. Heat the scallops in the steam.

2 Meanwhile, place the sesame oil and soy sauce in a small pan and warm through. Lay the scallops on four plates and sprinkle over the sesame and soy sauce. Sprinkle over the coriander and spring onions and serve.

Nutrition notes per serving: *335 calories, Protein 24g, Carbohydrate 2g, Fat 26g, Saturated fat 4g, Fibre trace, Added sugar trace, Salt 0.69g.*

OYSTERS WITH BEURRE BLANC AND SPINACH

The oysters in this dish are hardly cooked at all.

Serves 4 as a starter

16 oysters

16 spinach leaves, stalks removed

25g/1oz shallot or onion, finely chopped

1 tbsp white wine vinegar

1 tbsp white wine

150g/5½oz unsalted butter, cut into small squares

1 Prepare a steamer to cook the oysters (See above). Thoroughly wash the oysters and steam for about 4 minutes. Remove and open, reserving the bottom shells and the liquor that comes out of them. Place the spinach leaves in the steamer and steam for 2 minutes.

2 In a small pan, place the shallot, vinegar, wine, 50ml/2fl oz water and the oyster juices. Simmer until reduced to about two tablespoons. Off the heat, whisk in the butter a little at a time, building up a light emulsion.

3 Preheat the grill. Lay a folded spinach leaf in each bottom shell and place in an ovenproof dish. Warm the spinach under the grill. Place the oysters on top, spoon over the beurre blanc and warm under the grill.

Nutrition notes per serving: *634 calories, Protein 13g, Carbohydrate 2g, Fat 63g, Saturated fat 39g, Fibre 3g, Added sugar 0.02g, Salt 1.48g.*

TIP

To open oysters: wrap one hand in a tea towel and place the oyster in it, put your hand on a work top, push the point of an oyster knife or small, thick-bladed knife into the hinge of the oyster and, using firm but not excessive pressure, work the knife backwards and forwards into the shell, breaking the hinge. As the hinge breaks, twist the point of the knife to lever the shell up, then slide the knife under the top shell to sever the ligament that joins the oyster to the shell. The ligament is slightly off to the right of centre of the oyster. Lift off the top shell keeping the bottom shell upright to avoid losing any of the juice.

Grills

GRILLED RED MULLET WITH AN AUBERGINE AND PESTO SALAD

A perfect combination of flavours. This dish has its roots in the cooking of Simon Hopkinson, who used to be the chef at Bibendum restaurant in London. Mullet has a special place in my affections, with its beautiful pink and yellow tinges and its firm flaky texture and taste somewhere between fish and shellfish.

Serves 4

½ aubergine, sliced into 4 x 1cm/½in slices

olive oil, for brushing

4 x 85–115g/3–4oz red mullet fillets

FOR THE PESTO

15g/½oz fresh basil leaves

2 large garlic cloves

175ml/6fl oz olive oil

15g/½oz Parmesan

15g/½oz pine nuts

FOR THE SALAD

85g/3oz mixed salad leaves

1 tomato, peeled, seeded and chopped

1 tsp Lemon olive oil (See Tip, page 20)

salt and freshly ground black pepper

1 Make the pesto: place all the ingredients in a liquidiser or food processor for about 10 seconds, then remove half the mixture and set aside; it should be fairly coarse. Process the remaining pesto until it is smooth.

2 Preheat the grill to high. Brush the aubergine slices liberally with olive oil and season with salt. Grill until just cooked through.

3 Brush the red mullet fillets with oil and season with salt and pepper. Grill for 2 minutes on each side.

4 Meanwhile, spread the aubergine slices with the coarse pesto and place under the grill until the pesto is warm, then place on four warmed plates with the red mullet fillets.

5 Toss the salad leaves with the tomato, lemon olive oil, salt and pepper and place a small pile on each plate. Spoon the smooth pesto around each plate, making sure some, but not all, trickles over the fillets, then serve.

Nutrition notes per serving: *487 calories, Protein 23g, Carbohydrate 3g, Fat 42g, Saturated fat 7g, Fibre 2g, Added sugar none, Salt 0.53g.*

TIP

Whole fish keep better than filleted fish. Once filleted, the cut surface tends to oxidise and turn an unappetising yellow colour. You can slow down this process. Place the fillets in a shallow dish and wrap both fish and dish in plastic film. Dot cubes of ice around the top of the plastic wrap and place the dish in the coldest part of the fridge. It is not worth keeping fish for more than a couple of days. If you are going to keep it any longer, you would probably do better to freeze it and use within a week or two.

MONKFISH WITH SAFFRON AND ROASTED PEPPER DRESSING

Like many of my recipes there's not a lot to this dish really, but that is all to the good, providing you have the very freshest of fish. This can also be cooked on the barbecue – light it 30–40 minutes before you intend to cook the monkfish.

Serves 4

25ml/1fl oz olive oil

1 tbsp finely chopped fresh thyme

4 x 200g/7oz monkfish fillets

salt and freshly ground black pepper

1.2 litre/2 pint measuring jug loosely filled with salad leaves

1 tbsp Lemon olive oil
(See Tip, page 20)

good pinch sea salt, preferably coarse

FOR THE ROASTED PEPPER DRESSING

600ml/1 pint Fish stock (page 62)

90ml/3fl oz dry vermouth

large pinch saffron

2 red peppers

90ml/3fl oz virgin olive oil

1 tbsp balsamic vinegar or sherry vinegar

1 tsp unsalted butter

1   Make the sauce: place the fish stock, vermouth and saffron in a small pan and simmer to reduce in volume by three-quarters, then remove from the heat.

2   Roast the red peppers by putting them on a tray (you don't need to coat them with any oil) and charring under a grill, or in a hot oven, until the skins are blistered. Leave to cool, cut in half, remove the seeds, take off the skins and finely chop the flesh. Mix together the virgin olive oil and vinegar, then season with half a teaspoon of salt and some pepper and set aside.

3   Mix together the olive oil, thyme, salt and pepper and brush over the monkfish fillets. Cook in a very hot cast-iron ribbed grill pan or over the barbecue for about 10 minutes. Turn over frequently to prevent burning.

4   Return the fish stock and saffron to the heat, add the chopped peppers and olive oil dressing and bring to a brisk boil. Check the sauce is pleasantly strong; it should taste tart but not too tart, salty but not too salty. If it does not, continue to reduce by rapid boiling to concentrate the flavour. Once you are satisfied, whisk in the butter to give the sauce a light amalgamation and remove from the heat.

5   Mix together the salad leaves, lemon olive oil and sea salt and place on four plates. Slice each monkfish fillet into four thick pieces on the slant and place on top of the leaves. Spoon the sauce around and serve.

Nutrition notes per serving: *456 calories, Protein 31g, Carbohydrate 7g, Fat 32g, Saturated fat 5g, Fibre 2g, Added sugar 1g, Salt 1.34g.*

TIP

Fifteen years ago nobody had ever heard of monkfish. Now it is extraordinarily popular. It is not, in fact, particularly well-flavoured but it has the most marvellous texture, making it one of the best fish for barbecuing. A very fine purple membrane covers a monkfish fillet and if your fishmonger has not removed it, take as much off as possible or it will cause the fillet to twist unattractively as it cooks.

CHAR-GRILLED SWORDFISH STEAKS WITH SALSA FRESCA

You can just as successfully use tuna or sea bass for this dish. The grilled fish steaks are served with a hot chilli sauce and an ice-cold salsa and dressed with a thin mayonnaise-based sauce from Mexico. Try to keep the avocado, cucumber and tomatoes roughly the same size when chopping. If the spring onions are large cut them into quarters lengthways before thinly slicing. If you don't want to go to the (not enormous) trouble of making the Salsa Fresca just grill some steaks of swordfish or tuna and serve with a pool of extra virgin olive oil. The flesh of both swordfish and tuna is compact and swordfish is ideal for cutting into thin steaks and grilling. Tuna is better when cut into thicker steaks and left a little underdone in the centre.

Serves 4

4 x 175g/6oz swordfish steaks

olive oil, for brushing

salt and freshly ground black pepper

FOR THE SALSA

1 green chilli, seeded and finely chopped

1 avocado, cut into 5mm/¼in dice

2 garlic cloves, finely chopped

3 spring onions, thinly sliced

½ cucumber, cut into 5mm/¼in dice

juice of 2 limes

2 under-ripe tomatoes, skinned, seeded and cut into 5mm/¼in dice

1 tbsp fresh coriander, roughly chopped

FOR THE SAUCE

4 green olives

4 heaped tbsp Olive oil mayonnaise (page 62)

50ml/2fl oz double cream

1   Keep all the prepared salsa ingredients cold, and separate until just before serving, then quickly mix together in a bowl and divide between four plates.

2   Make the sauce: cut the olive flesh from the stones in strips, then cut the strips into thin pine needle-sized shards. In a small pan, mix the mayonnaise, cream and 125ml/4fl oz warm water with the olive shards, then warm through. The sauce should be served warm, not hot.

3   Heat a cast-iron ribbed grill pan until very hot. Season the swordfish steaks and brush with olive oil. Grill for about 3 minutes on each side. Alternatively, you can cook the steaks on a barbecue. Lift onto the plates and spoon some of the sauce over the steaks and around the rest of the plates.

Nutrition notes per serving: *542 calories, Protein 41g, Carbohydrate 4g, Fat 40g, Saturated fat 8g, Fibre 2g, Added sugar none, Salt 0.87g.*

TIP

Barbecuing or char-grilling is one of my favourite ways of cooking fish. When barbecuing, don't be mean with the charcoal. Build up a really good fire, then let it die down. When barbecuing you cook on the residual heat to achieve the best results because the great enemy of good barbecue cooking is flame. What you really need is very hot ash because then, providing that the barbecue is very hot (and therefore the barbecue bars are very hot) and the fish or even fillets are well oiled, they shouldn't stick. A lot of cookery books suggest you shouldn't season anything before you put it on a charcoal grill because you won't get a crisp char-grilled surface. This is total rubbish; it works perfectly and anything cooked on a grill should be pre-seasoned.

CAUTION! The sauce in this recipe contains raw eggs.

GRILLED SCORED PLAICE WITH GARLIC, OREGANO AND LEMON JUICE

This is good served with a bowl of chips (See Tip) and a dressed soft lettuce salad.

Serves 4

4 x 450g/1lb whole plaice, cleaned

1 small red pepper, skinned, seeded and chopped into 3mm/⅛in dice

½ mild red chilli, seeded and finely chopped

50ml/2fl oz virgin olive oil

1 large garlic clove, finely chopped

1 tsp chopped fresh oregano or ½ tsp dried

1 tsp salt

pinch of freshly ground black pepper

juice of ¼ lemon

1 Cut off the fins with a pair of scissors and trim the tail. Make a deep cut down the back of each fish from head to tail. Then, make a series of diagonal cuts across from this cut to the sides so that the slashes look like the veins of a leaf. Turn the fish over and do the same on the other side.

2 Add the red pepper to a bowl with the chilli, olive oil, garlic, oregano, salt, black pepper and lemon juice to make the marinade.

3 One hour before cooking, coat both sides of the fish with the marinade, making sure that it spreads into the slashes. Preheat grill to maximum. Grill the fish for 5 minutes on each side starting with the light side.

Nutrition notes per serving: 265 calories, Protein 34g, Carbohydrate 2g, Fat 14g, Saturated fat 2g, Fibre trace, Added sugar none, Salt 1.81g.

TIP

I have never forgotten the wonderful earthy flavour of some chips eaten in a taverna in Paxos, Greece, caused by not being too fastidious with the peeling. Just roughly peel some potatoes (such as Maris Piper) leaving on some of the peel, then cut into large, irregular chips and deep-fry in hot oil until golden.

CHAR-GRILLED SQUID WITH A PEPPER MARINADE

This dish is equally delicious made with cuttlefish. Serve with lemon wedges.

Serves 4

½ tsp each of black and Szechuan peppercorns, ground together

1 red chilli, seeded and chopped

50ml/2fl oz virgin olive oil

juice of ½ lemon

½ tsp salt

1 tbsp dark soy sauce

1 garlic clove, finely chopped

350g/12oz cleaned squid

85g/3oz rocket leaves

1 Make the marinade: combine the pepper, chilli, olive oil, lemon juice, salt, soy sauce and garlic.

2 Cut the bodies of the squid into 7.5cm/3in pieces and each bunch of tentacles in half. Place in the marinade for 30 minutes, turning once or twice.

3 Remove the squid from the marinade and barbecue or cook in the grill pan for 1 minute, then turn and cook for another minute. Place the squid on the rocket and drizzle over remaining marinade.

Nutrition notes per serving: 160 calories, Protein 15g, Carbohydrate 2g, Fat 10g, Saturated fat 1g, Fibre trace, Added sugar none, Salt 1.04g.

GRATIN OF SEAFOOD

Last time I was in France I chose a seafood gratin from a Sunday lunch menu in a small seaside town in the south, not because I was really enthusiastic about the idea, but because there was not really anything else very interesting on the menu. I had totally forgotten how fantastic that combination of seafood, cream and cheese can be.

Serves 4

450g/1lb cooked prawns
in their shells

½ onion, roughly chopped

70g/2½oz butter

1 tbsp cognac

600ml/1 pint Fish stock (page 62)

50ml/2fl oz white wine

2 tomatoes, roughly chopped

900g/2lb fresh mussels, cleaned

2 shallots, finely chopped

20g/¾oz plain flour

150ml/¼ pint double cream

1 tbsp chopped fresh parsley

salt and freshly ground black pepper

juice ½ lemon

8 prepared scallops (See Tip)

175g/6oz skinless haddock fillet,
cut into small chunks

115g/4oz button mushrooms, sliced

115g/4oz white crab meat, fresh
if possible

115g/4oz Gruyère, Emmental,
Fontina or Jarlsberg cheese,
coarsely grated

¼ tsp paprika

pinch cayenne pepper

1   Peel the prawns, reserving the heads and shells. Fry the onion in 15g/½oz of butter until soft. Add the prawn shells and cognac and fry for 1–2 minutes. Add the fish stock, wine and tomatoes and simmer for 20 minutes.

2   Add the mussels to the pan, cover and cook over a high heat for 3–4 minutes until they have opened. Discard any that do not open. Tip everything into a colander or large sieve set over a bowl – you should be left with 600ml/1 pint stock. If there is any less, make it up with a little fish stock; any more and you need to return it to the pan and boil it until it is reduced to the required amount. Remove the mussel meats from the shells and set aside with the peeled prawns. Discard everything else.

3   Fry the shallots in 25g/1oz of butter until soft. Stir in the flour and cook for 1 minute, stirring. Remove the pan from the heat and gradually stir in the stock. Return to the heat and bring to the boil, stirring. Stir in the cream and simmer very gently for 10 minutes until the sauce has thickened and it coats the back of a wooden spoon. Add the parsley, season with salt and pepper and add a little lemon juice to taste.

4   Preheat the grill to high. Melt the remaining butter. Scatter the scallops, haddock and mushrooms over the base of a large gratin dish. Brush with the butter, season and grill for 2 minutes. Remove the dish, turn the scallops and grill for a further 2 minutes.

5   Add the prawns, mussels and white crab meat to the dish and spoon over the sauce. Sprinkle with the cheese, dust with the paprika and cayenne pepper and grill for another 1–2 minutes until golden and bubbling.

Nutrition notes per serving: *689 calories, Protein 59g, Carbohydrate 8g, Fat 45g, Saturated fat 26g, Fibre 1g, Added sugar none, Salt 4.70g.*

TIP

Scallops are one of our most delicious shellfish – sweet and firm and relatively cheap. Only buy fresh scallops and steer clear of frozen ones, since they have often been soaked in water before freezing to increase their size and make the price seem more attractive. When they thaw, the water drains out of them along with a great deal of their flavour.

Salads

SKATE MAYONNAISE WITH A VEGETABLE SALAD

Having no bones and a firm texture, skate is an ideal fish for poaching and serving cold in a salad.

Serves 4

1 quantity Court-bouillon (page 62)

675g/1½lb skate (See Tip)

FOR THE VEGETABLE SALAD

30ml/1fl oz groundnut oil

55g/2oz each of celery, carrot and leek, cut into 5cm/2in matchsticks

30ml/1fl oz white wine

salt and freshly ground black pepper

55g/2oz French beans, cut into 5cm/2in lengths

55g/2oz mangetout

8 lettuce leaves from the heart of a lettuce

FOR THE MAYONNAISE

115g/4oz Olive oil mayonnaise (page 62)

85g/3oz tomato, peeled, seeded and roughly chopped

1 avocado, chopped

115g/4oz cooked potato, diced

1   Bring the court-bouillon to a gentle simmer, add the skate and poach for 15–20 minutes. Leave to cool in the liquid.

2   Make the vegetable salad: heat the oil in a shallow pan and gently cook the celery, carrot and leek for 1 minute. Add the wine, salt and pepper and cook until the wine has boiled off completely. Turn out on to a plate and chill.

3   Bring a pan of salted water to the boil and blanch the beans and mangetout for 30 seconds, then plunge into cold water. Drain through a colander and mix with the other vegetables (together with the eight lettuce leaves), then season.

4   Remove the skin from the skate and lift the flesh away from the cartilage-like bones. Flake into pieces and mix with the olive oil mayonnaise, tomato, avocado and potato. Check seasoning. Serve with lettuce leaves and the vegetable salad, garnished with the lettuce leaves.

Nutrition notes per serving: *510 calories, Protein 25g, Carbohydrate 10g, Fat 41g, Saturated fat 5g, Fibre 4g, Added sugar none, Salt 2g.*

TIP

The wings of skate are the only parts sold and are normally skinned before sale. I would suggest that, if possible, you should go for skate wings weighing between 450–900g/1–2lb. Any larger and the skate becomes rather coarse; smaller, and they can be a bit fiddly. To all intents and purposes, although they are different species, skate, thornback ray, starry ray and spotted ray are normally sold by fishmongers as skate. The best eating of all the skate or rays is the thornback ray. Be a bit careful if you happen to get hold of a whole fish, though, because they're called thornback rays for a reason.

CAUTION! This recipe contains raw eggs.

GRILLED TUNA SALAD WITH GUACAMOLE

This dish comes from the Fifth Floor Restaurant in Harvey Nichols department store in London. The idea that raw tuna is cooked on a charcoal grill so briefly that only the outside is coloured and caramelised and inside practically raw has been much copied and adapted, especially to meat such as fillet steak. But I know from talking to the chef, Henry Harris, at the Fifth Floor, that he was the one who brought the dish to England from California, and jolly good for him. This is not his exact recipe. I much prefer to get enthusiastic about a dish in someone else's restaurant than attempt to copy it.

Serves 4

450g/1lb tuna fillet

oil, for brushing

sea salt and freshly ground black pepper

4 fresh coriander sprigs, to garnish

FOR THE GUACAMOLE

1 large avocado, roughly chopped (See Tip)

1 green chilli, seeded

juice of 1 lime

2 spring onions, chopped

1 tbsp chopped fresh coriander

3 tbsp vegetable oil

½ tsp salt

FOR THE SOY SAUCE DRESSING

1 tbsp dark soy sauce

1 spring onion, finely chopped

¼ green chilli, seeded and chopped

juice and grated rind of ½ lime

½ stick lemon grass, finely sliced

1 tsp chopped fresh root ginger

1 Heat a charcoal grill or cast-iron ribbed grill pan until it is very hot. Brush the tuna with oil and sprinkle liberally with salt and pepper. Blacken the fillet on the grill for 2–3 minutes, turning to colour all over. Remember the centre of the tuna should remain raw. Remove from the grill or pan and season again. Leave to cool completely.

2 In a food processor, blend together all the guacamole ingredients until smooth. Mix together all the dressing ingredients.

3 Slice the tuna into 5mm/¼in slices and arrange on four cold plates. The slices should slightly overlap and be to the side of the plates. Place a spoonful of the guacamole on each plate, again slightly to the side (offsetting food on plates makes it look more natural). Add a generous pool of dressing, then garnish the guacamole with fresh coriander.

Nutrition notes per serving: *306 calories, Protein 26g, Carbohydrate 2g, Fat 22g, Saturated fat 2g, Fibre 2g, Added sugar none, Salt 0.98g.*

TIP

Never prepare avocados too far in advance as their flesh discolours badly once it is exposed to air. Cut the fruit in half, then ease the pieces apart. Some stones come out easily. If it doesn't stab the stone with a point of an old knife, then pull free. Sprinkle with a little of the lime juice if not processing immediately. Then remove the skin just before using.

SALAD OF PRAWNS, ROCKET AND PARMA HAM

All the flavours in this salad are interesting on their own, but drawn together with some good olive oil they produce an effect greater than the sum of their parts.

Serves 4

55g/2oz rocket leaves

6 very thin slices Parma ham

115g/4oz large cooked peeled prawns, defrosted if frozen

4 tbsp extra virgin olive oil

freshly ground black pepper

1 Divide the rocket between four cold plates. Tear the Parma ham into pieces about 5cm/2in across and arrange among the leaves.

2 Scatter over the prawns, then drizzle one tablespoon of olive oil over each salad, grind over some black pepper and serve.

Nutrition notes per serving: *179 calories, Protein 14g, Carbohydrate 0.06g, Fat 14g, Saturated fat 2g, Fibre trace, Added sugar none, Salt 2.26g.*

HOT MACKEREL SALAD WITH LETTUCE, LEMON GRASS AND CORIANDER

This recipe is from Laos in South-east Asia. The traditional way to eat the grilled fish and dressing is with a pile of whole lettuce leaves. The fillet is removed from the mackerel, laid on a lettuce leaf, and some of the dressing poured over. Coriander is sprinkled on top and the whole thing is wrapped up and eaten like a pancake.

Serves 4

4 mackerel (large for a main course, small for a starter)

vegetable oil, for brushing

salt and freshly ground black pepper

½ iceberg lettuce, thinly sliced, or 1 whole lettuce for pancakes

FOR THE DRESSING

30ml/1fl oz Thai fish sauce (*nam pla*)

1 green chilli, seeded and finely chopped

1 lemon grass stick, thinly sliced

Finely sliced rind and juice of 1 lime

½ tsp sugar

1 tbsp roughly chopped fresh coriander, plus about 20 leaves, to garnish

1 Preheat the grill. Slash the fish diagonally three times on each side, cutting right through to the bone. Brush with oil and season. Grill for 4 minutes on each side or until cooked (See Tip).

2 Meanwhile, place 150ml/¼ pint water and all the dressing ingredients, except the coriander, in a pan and warm through (don't boil) over a moderate heat. Add the chopped coriander just before taking off the heat.

3 If serving the mackerel whole with the salad, divide the lettuce between the plates and place the mackerel on top, then pour over the dressing and garnish with coriander.

4 If serving lettuce pancakes, serve the fish, the sauce, whole coriander leaves and lettuce leaves separately.

Nutrition notes per serving: *473 calories, Protein 39g, Carbohydrate 3g, Fat 34g, Saturated fat 8g, Fibre trace, Added sugar 1g, Salt 1.70g.*

TIP

The best way to eat mackerel is to cook it on the day it is caught. Make sure it has some traces of blue or green in its skin. If it looks grey it won't be interesting to eat. To check the mackerel is cooked, lift up the gill covers. If there is no trace of pink left, then it is done.

Vegetable Dishes

GRILLED VEGETABLES

Serves 4

1 aubergine, sliced

2 courgettes, sliced

2 red onions, cut into quarters lengthways

1 fennel bulb, sliced lengthways

2 red peppers, seeded and cut into 8 pieces

30ml/1fl oz olive oil

pinch of dried marjoram

salt and freshly ground black pepper

1   Preheat the grill, or a barbecue to high. Place all the ingredients in a bowl and stir to coat vegetables evenly with the oil, marjoram and seasoning. Grill or barbecue until cooked through.

Nutrition notes per serving:
126 calories, Protein 4g, Carbohydrate 13g, Fat 7g, Saturated fat 1g, Fibre 6g, Added sugar none, Salt 0.28g.

STIR-FRIED SPINACH WITH GARLIC, GINGER AND CHILLI

Serves 4

30ml/1fl oz vegetable oil

1 tsp finely chopped garlic

1 tsp finely chopped fresh root ginger

225g/8oz fresh spinach leaves

pinch of chilli powder

1 tsp Thai fish sauce (nam pla) or anchovy paste

1   Heat the oil in a wok or large frying pan and when hot add the garlic and ginger. Stir-fry quickly until they start to brown.
2   Add the spinach and turn in the oil for 30 seconds. Add the chilli powder and fish sauce. Reduce the heat to low, cover and cook for 1 minute, then serve.

Nutrition notes per serving:
67 calories, Protein 2g, Carbohydrate 2g, Fat 6g, Saturated fat 1g, Fibre 1g, Added sugar none, Salt 0.34g.

GRILLED POTATOES

Serves 4

450g/1lb large potatoes, cut into 5mm/1/4in slices lengthways

50ml/2fl oz virgin olive oil

salt and freshly ground black pepper

1   Boil the potatoes in salted water until tender, then drain. Preheat the grill to high.
2   Lay the potatoes on a grill tray and brush liberally on both sides with olive oil. Season with black pepper and grill until beginning to turn brown.

Nutrition notes per serving:
168 calories, Protein 2g, Carbohydrate 19g, Fat 9g, Saturated fat 1g, Fibre 1g, Added sugar none, Salt 0.27g.

Basic Recipes

FISH STOCK ✳

You can make good fish stock out of any fish bones except oily ones. Although a precise recipe is given here, the quantities are actually not very important. By cooking the stock twice, more flavour can be extracted from the fish bones and vegetables. I have not included salt because normally the stock will be greatly reduced and so could become too salty. The seasoning should be added after the stock has been reduced.

Makes 1.2 litres/2 pints

1.3kg/3lb fish bones, including heads

handful of fresh white button mushrooms, sliced

1 large onion, chopped

1 large leek, chopped

1 large carrot, chopped

1 celery stick, including the leafy top, sliced

1　Place the fish bones in 1.7 litres/ 3 pints of water and bring to the boil. Simmer for 20 minutes, then strain through a strainer lined with muslin.

2　Return the stock to the pan and add the vegetables. Bring to the boil and simmer for 45 minutes. Strain again. Store in a covered container in the fridge for up to four days.

✳ *Store it in small quantities in the freezer.*

COURT-BOUILLON

This is a general purpose poaching liquid for skate, salmon and any occasion when you want to cook fish with plenty of flavour. After poaching the fish, you can use the bouillon and vegetables as part of the stock for fish soup. You can also strain it for use as an unreduced fish stock.

Makes 1.2 litres/2 pints

300ml/½ pint dry cider

90ml/3fl oz white wine vinegar

2 fresh or dried bay leaves

12 black peppercorns

1 onion, roughly chopped

2 carrots, roughly chopped

2 celery sticks, roughly chopped

1 tsp salt

1　Place all the ingredients in a large pan with 1.2 litres/2 pints of water and bring to the boil. Simmer for 30 minutes.

2　To complete the infusion of flavours, leave to cool before using. Store as for Fish stock.

OLIVE OIL MAYONNAISE

This recipe for mayonnaise is one of the utmost simplicity. You will find that using best extra virgin olive oil produces a waxy, slightly green finish which tastes bitter. Too strong you may think but, like most sauces, mayonnaise should be a bit strong on its own. When combined with the rest of the dish, such as poached salmon or sea trout, everything falls delightfully into place.

Serves 4

2 egg yolks

2 tsp white wine vinegar

½ tsp salt

300ml/½ pint extra virgin olive oil

1　Make sure all the ingredients are at room temperature before beginning. Place the egg yolks, vinegar and salt in a mixing bowl, then place the bowl on a tea towel to stop it slipping.

2　Using a wire whisk, beat the oil into the egg mixture a little at a time until you have incorporated it all. Once you have added about the same volume of oil as the original mixture of egg yolks and vinegar, add the oil more quickly.

CAUTION! This recipe contains raw eggs.

INDEX